Khudi Bari — A social project by Marina Tabassum Architects

and its journey from Dhaka to Weil am Rhein

Vitra
Design
Museum

The Bangladeshi architect Marina Tabassum's Khudi Bari (Little House) was installed on the Vitra Campus in summer 2024. While we might call it a shed on stilts rather than a house, for those living in the floodplains of Bangladesh, it is a significant improvement over what they had before, and the cost of a Khudi Bari is under 500 US dollars.

I first encountered a Khudi Bari in March 2023 at an exhibition of Marina Tabassum's work at the Munich Architecture Museum. I was struck by its simplicity, intelligent construction and surprising beauty. I felt that a Khudi Bari would offer a great lesson and asked Marina if she would be willing to build one on the Vitra Campus in Weil am Rhein. She agreed, and soon afterwards, work on the logistics began. The structural elements and major materials would be sent from Bangladesh in a container. They arrived in spring 2024 and were assembled in a collaborative effort between local artisans, architect Arman Abedin from the Marina Tabassum office, and Vitra architects Christian Germadnik and Abel Rodríguez. The chosen site was in an area next to the Oudolf Garden and Renzo Piano's little Diogene house.

What purpose does an emergency structure from Bangladesh have on the Vitra Campus? Some might view it as indulging in exoticism, but this is far from our intention. We have been interested in emergency shelters for a long time. In the Vitra Design Museum's exhibition on Jean Prouvé in 2006, his demountable buildings designed for disaster victims from Lorraine at the end of World War II were prominently featured, and our collection includes a Maison Démontable 6×6 by Prouvé. On the Vitra Campus in 1995, we joined together with Shigeru Ban to experiment with cardboard tubes as a building material for emergency shelters. More recently, I was involved in a publication on Swiss vernacular architecture, which highlights the merits of building under challenging constraints.

The Khudi Bari offers lessons on multiple levels. It demonstrates that architects can have an important social role, and that working under rigid constraints can produce an architecture of resilience with its own beauty. It is also a reminder of climate change. In the coming years, our region will more frequently experience periods of extreme heat and flooding. While the construction of Khudi Baris will not be our solution, we must rethink architecture and accept new constraints.

ROLF FEHLBAUM

Attention Matters

ANDRÉ TAVARES

An architect's biography is often split between the author's subjectivity and the collective endeavour of their work. Like many of today's architects, Marina Tabassum was trained in a very twentieth-century manner, where the genius author as social visionary is presented as the ideal form-maker to mould society's urban aesthetics. While such pedagogical strategies may be seen as a means to expand the imagination, they instil in architects a wilfulness and illusion of control, with outcomes that often collide with subtle social and ecological equilibriums. This can be frustrating for architects – often pigeonholed as designers for wealthy clients – but its effect is even more consequential when the singular nature of architectural knowledge is detached from major contemporary challenges such as climate change and social justice. Among architects, the split between subjectivity and equity had a major impact on the twenty-first-century definition of the profession, with opposing visions laying claim to architecture either as a tool for social design or as an autonomous field for intellectual creation. Tabassum's journey demonstrates that subjectivity and equity can coexist, nurturing each other and infusing design with optimism. Without cynicism or naivety, her accomplishments have brought new insights relevant to overcoming the many impasses faced by the architectural profession.

Tabassum works in Dhaka, the capital of Bangladesh. Situated where the Ganges and Brahmaputra rivers flow into the Bay of Bengal, and independent since 1971, Bangladesh is home to over 150 million people. It is a water-rich landscape, with 700 rivers flowing across it, with lakes, dams, canals and wetlands carrying water throughout the year. A flatland of clay and sediments, most of its areas are only a few metres above sea level, prone to flooding and sensitive to any rise in ocean levels. In addition, the large influx of rural inhabitants into the districts of the capital that are home to the textile industry made Dhaka one of the world's largest metropolises, with automobile infrastructure and predatory building developers gobbling up the urban fabric. Within this context, Tabassum developed an architectural practice that escapes the metropolitan pressure and offers lines of thought for addressing contemporary predicaments such as climate change, forced migration and sustainable building culture.

Abdur Rouf Tower, Bijoy Nagar, Dhaka, 2015/2019–2022

Photo City Syntax

She has designed and built several private and public buildings in Dhaka, devising adequate natural ventilation systems to counter the tropical monsoon conditions and achieving good levels of comfort with passive means. These forms combine brick and reinforced concrete in agile compositions, and it is the sophisticated manipulation of banal resources that gives the buildings their special quality. Flooring made of cement and recycled glass marbles has a unique texture and light reflections, while the joinery of a skilful carpenter recalls ancient Venetian woodwork, and a rich textile element adds emphasis to a pleasing colour spectrum. These combinations can take on an urban dimension, as is the case with the former home of the Hamidur Rahman family. The lot occupies a strategic position between the river and the busy streets, within an industrialized commercial district. The remnants of the existing structures were preserved and augmented by new constructions, including small-scale pavilions that reorganize the existing terrain into a hospitable garden. The new and old materials enter into dialogue with each other, while the new constructions are appropriately scaled to suit each part of the ensemble. It is this combinatory sense that Tabassum brings to her work as an architect, infusing the complex urban fabric of Bangladeshi cities with attention and objectivity. As busy as she is, Tabassum maintains a small architectural studio, carefully selecting her commissions to preserve the optimum relationship between the many people involved in the construction of the built environment. And alongside her professional practice, Tabassum carries on nonprofit activities as the instigator and chair of the

"The mosque is a refuge in a dense urban neighbourhood. Clarity of space, devoid of hierarchy, is tantamount. Instead of glorifying symbolic features, it felt right to focus on the spirituality of the space. Light became a major element of the design."

MARINA TABASSUM

Foundation for Architecture and Community Equity (FACE), which has given rise to such projects as the Khudi Bari initiative.

Bait Ur Rouf Mosque was Tabassum's breakthrough project. Commissioned by her late grandmother, it occupies a site on the northern periphery of Dhaka in a formerly agricultural area that is now an expanding and dense residential neighbourhood with significant infrastructure deficiency and a lack of social areas. Devoid of ritualistic and symbolic attributes, the mosque presents a gentle urban profile attuned to old Bengali constructions, their presence dignified by the solid mass of bricks that give shape to elegant volumes. Building the mosque was a unique occasion for Tabassum, enabling her to apply the broad experience that defines her as an architect. To resolve the misalignment between the urban setting and the orientation towards the *qibla* required for the congregational room, the design combines three geometric forms: an outside square rotated 13 degrees in relation to an inner square, intersected by a cylindrical volume connecting the inner space for prayer with its civic exterior. The bricks are laid in such a way as to create screens with strategic transparencies, with the half-moon cuts between the circle and the squares allowing natural light into the hall, and forms and materials giving the surfaces a porosity capable of bridging inside and outside areas, while providing natural ventilation and emphasizing the movement of light during the day. Building the mosque was a challenge, and in addition to the engagement with the community, it required the architect to fundraise for the project. Geometry and participation became entangled in her practice as she created a space of congregation, combining religious, educational and social functions, making architecture a local point of reference.

Bait Ur Rouf Mosque, Faidabad, Dhaka, 2005–2012

Photo Sandro di Carlo Darsa

The mosque marked a significant move away from her debut project, Dhaka's Independence Museum and Monument, whose history is imbricated in her own past. The celebrated memorial, which she designed at

"The project demanded an investigation into contemplation and timelessness. The independence of Bangladesh is a tale of duality: independence gained through selfless sacrifice in a brutal war. Two columns of light define the two events. One is set on the plaza as a beacon of hope; the other is a column of water absorbing the pain of loss. One is not complete without the other."

MARINA TABASSUM

→
Independence Museum,
Dhaka, 1997–2009
URBANA: Kashef Chowdhury,
Marina Tabassum,
Suhrawary Udyan

Photo Sandro di Carlo Darsa

↓
Independence Monument,
Dhaka, 1997–2009
URBANA: Kashef Chowdhury,
Marina Tabassum,
Suhrawary Udyan

Photo Asif Salman

the age of twenty-eight with her then partner Kashef Chowdhury, recalled a bloody war that marked the end of a long struggle rooted in the partition of the Indian subcontinent in 1947. The memorial evokes the silence and introspective materiality of modern architecture, notably Louis Kahn's neighbouring National Assembly Building and the strong Bengali modern architectural legacy. A sequence of ramps, curves, walkways and light shafts creates a powerful sensorial experience emphasized by the textures of concrete and the reflections of glass, shaping the monumental tower of light. This exercise in translating memories and history into architectural experience avoided nostalgia and nationalistic celebrations and proved to be a starting point for discovering sensitive forms of architectural expression.

Gaining international recognition with her work, Tabassum was invited to teach in the United States, Canada and the Netherlands and to lecture or participate in architecture exhibitions all over the world. She managed to make teaching an extension of her practice, filling design studios with the optimistic enthusiasm of architectural students and bringing their ideas, research and scholarship into dialogue with professional concerns. Whereas American or European cities face different immediate challenges in comparison to the Bay of Bengal, the core of the architectural profession is not dissimilar, and the planetary predicaments are shared. Tabassum brought international students to Bangladesh, where they engaged in participatory exercises leading to a significant accumulation and exchange of knowledge. One such experience was Panigram Resort, an eco-tourism project built in a rural region near Sunderban. The group of architects got involved with the local communities, learning their crafts and skills, understanding how to build with earth in a floodplain area, and developing housing possibilities in a context of resource scarcity. The experiments required a balance between hands-on activities and intellectual preoccupations, a strategy for bridging the distance between Western-minded design prej-

"Rural Bangladesh is uniquely beautiful – the soul of the delta land. It felt like a crime to invade the silence with the roaring noise of architecture. Panigram offered an opportunity to bring back the lost pride and belief in the wisdom of the land crafted over hundreds of years of dwelling in the delta."

MARINA TABASSUM

Panigram Resort, Taherpur,
Jessore, 2012–2018

Photo Marina Tabassum

Panigram Resort, Taherpur,
Jessore, 2012–2018

Photo Afzalur Rahman Xelon

udices and objective planetary needs. Panigram Resort demonstrates how vernacular techniques can keep pace with contemporary requirements for comfort, and how design can mitigate the harsh disruptions that result when tourism discovers rural areas. Analogous to the local housing types, the resort bungalows form courtyards, and the sweeping forms of the pavilions are distributed along the mangrove thickets. The walls and floors are made of sun-dried earth, covered by bamboo-thatched roofs, the clay mass regulating the interior climate. By exposing her students to unique forms of knowledge, experimental approaches and engagement with communities and traditional technologies, Tabassum merges the large set of competencies that are synthesized in her work: understanding architecture as a collaborative practice for a distinct location.

What makes Tabassum's architecture so special? One hypothesis is attention to architecture as a collective endeavour without losing the author's subjectivity. On the one hand, there are the materials. Bangladesh is a country of clay; hence, brick is one of her chosen materials. She also builds in bamboo, a lightweight and high-performance material that is easy to source outside the main industrialized supply chains. On the other hand, there is geometry, the architect's tool for engaging with gravity, structural design and the shaping of forms. We tend to perceive geometry as a set of fixed rules, yet its output is dynamic, as dynamic as the architecture of the present needs to be. Attention is a tool for balancing equity with subjectivity, material with geometry. When speaking on the variety of her projects, Tabassum emphasizes not only how each of the actors involved in the process contributes to the outcome – from those sourcing materials to the users, from the engineers to the contractors and self-builders, from authorities to relief and funding agencies – but also how architects navigate within these multiple contexts to mobilize resources and respond to specific needs. Tabassum's architecture is special because it reveals attention, a care that matters in obtaining the kind of dynamic responses we need today. Geometry might be the tool, but attention to the power of collective knowledge, along with the capacity to orchestrate such knowledge, is Tabassum's greatest

↓
Marina Tabassum during the construction of a Khudi Bari in Char Hijla, Barishal, Meghna River Delta, 2021

Photo Asif Salman/MTA

contribution to the discipline. Her works, such as the Khudi Bari, are expressions of a broader ambition – an architecture that is subtle, dynamic and capable of responding to our times.

■

Khudi Bari: An Architecture of Transition

MARINA TABASSUM

"Man fears time; time fears the pyramids." The splendour of Egypt is the ultimate testament of resistance and perpetuity: weathering the storms of humanity and cultural changes through millennia, the pyramids have defied time.

Architecture of power – be it political, economic, cultural or religious – has sought permanence throughout history irrespective of geography, culture and civilization. The yearning for eternal continuity or the urge to defy gravity or to assert exclusivity compelled every civilization in history to seek permanence through architecture. In the Ganges delta, permanence came in the form of brick. The fragile alluvium was shaped and baked to perfection, adding to the richness of the legacy and power of architecture. The Buddhist monasteries of Pundranagar dating back to the third century BC were built with bricks; the Hindu temple of Kantanagar showcases the finest terracotta works depicting the mythologies of Ramayana and Mahabharata. In appreciation of the richness of the brick building traditions of the delta, the mosques of the Sultanates in the fourteenth century drew on that heritage.

Conversely, the architecture of human dwelling in the delta never sought permanence, frequently adapting to changes by employing organic, perishable, locally sourced materials. North of the Padma river, the Barind from the Pleistocene era boasts two-storey buildings made with mud. The soil in the matured deltas to the south of the Padma is

essentially alluvium; as such the houses take the form of small huts gathered around a courtyard, mud being the predominant vernacular construction material. People do not aspire for their own dwellings to differ from those of their neighbours. Values are rooted in homogeneity and a communal way of life. Anonymous architecture embodies centuries of accumulated tangible and intangible knowledge about the connection between humans and the environment. The formation of spontaneous human settlements is influenced by the natural environment, geography, climate, available resources and skills. There is inherent wisdom embedded in living symbiotically with nature.

Impermanence is not only an aspect of human dwelling, but is also intrinsic to the dynamic nature of the Ganges delta. The interplay of erosion and accretion is a unique phenomenon that has shaped the lives of Bengalis who inhabit the fragile land at the confluence of three major rivers, Padma, Meghna and Jamuna. There exists a duality of joy and untold torments each year for a large number of people living along the banks of Bangladesh's watercourses. The water level rises during the monsoon season between June and October. The tributary streams carrying excess snowmelt from the Himalayas also inflate and expand the fluvial territory, causing the banks to erode and shift.

(→ p. 30)

In the flux of this land–water matrix, the houses move, and the villages also move along with the bazaars. In some cases, the entire town is relocated. Some families have moved three or four times, and some have ultimately settled in the urban slums to seek a livelihood after losing the means to start anew. Many such stories of complex existence and unending negotiation between human and nature were documented through MTA's research for the Sharjah Architecture Triennial in 2019. Our investigation into land ownership and precarious inheritance laws offered a closer look at human life and longing subject to the transient geoformation accelerated by the effects of rising sea levels.

↑
Source: https://www.bproperty.com/blog/traditional-bengali-village-house/

←
Shompur Mohabihar
Photo Md. Ahsanul Haque Nayem

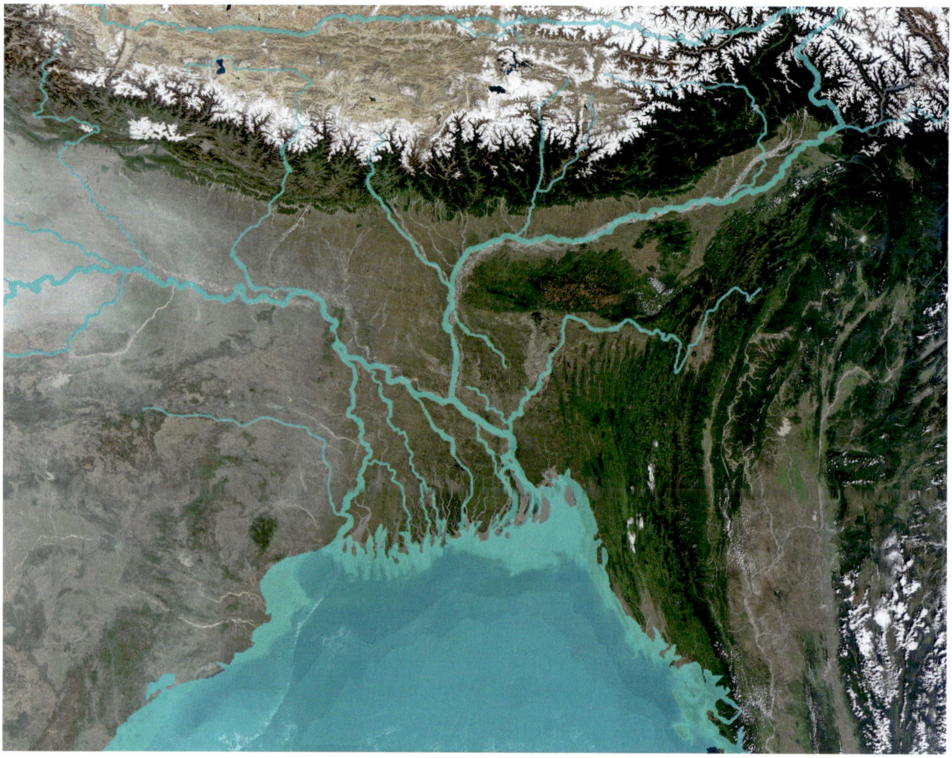

Source: NASA

The site specificity of the mud houses is not based on rational or objective conditions in the active delta, which is in constant flux. The houses along the banks of the Padma and Meghna rivers are adapted to a flat-pack system with a wooden frame and corrugated metal sheets. This vernacular dwelling type allows mobility, thereby addressing the impermanent nature of the delta. In the wake of significant erosion, the houses can be disassembled and moved to safer locations. In the region of Munshiganj, Dohar Bikrampur and Lauhajang along the river Padma, this typology is visible in its full abundance. The houses are available readymade and can also be ordered through the local market. Based on the current market price, a basic house costs between 1,500 and 4,000 US dollars. For low-income communities that have lost their homesteads to the rivers, this is not an affordable option.

The tidal dynamics and low currents during the dry season form sedimentation locally known as char. Fishermen and boatmen are the first to identify it, and word spreads quickly around the mainland. The alluvium of the delta is fertile ground. If a char does not erode during the first four years of its existence, it can then be used for fishing and cultivation. It is these possibilities that encourage landless families and river nomads, who are locally called charua, to migrate to the newly emerged land. Furthermore, the Meghna estuary is abundant with the Hilsa fish that swim upstream to spawn. Hilsa fish are inextricably intertwined with Bengali culture, generating significant economic opportunity that compels people to live in this precarious landscape.

As settlers negotiate ownership of the newly surfaced char, nature silently steps in with tall grass (hogla) that anchors the soil. Mudskipper fish are the first to appear, attracting birds in their wake. Crabs and shellfish colonies emerge from the riverbed. While fishermen start to stake boundaries (ghers) around the char, buffalos are brought in for grazing. For landless, ultra-low-income people, chars offer some years of relief as they settle down with their family, fishing and cultivating the land. A shack made from tall grass costs nothing but provides a roof overhead. The transitory nature of these treadable parts of the river does not allow

←
Aerial view of Char Shildoho, Jamalpur, 2021
Photo City Syntax

Illustration Sabiha Haque/MTA

HUMAN
BUFFALO
BALI HASH
HILSHA
CRAB
MOSQUITOES
DRAGON FLY
SHELL FISH
FALL ARMY WARM
HOGLA(Typha elephantiana)
SHRIMP
MUD SKIPPER

←
Khudi Bari in Char Hijla, Barishal, Meghna River Delta, 2021
Photo Asif Salman/MTA

↓
Khudi Bari in Char Hijla, Barishal, Meghna River Delta, 2021
Photo Asif Salman/MTA

Khudi Bari in Char Hijla, Barishal, Meghna River Delta, 2021
Photo Asif Salman/MTA

for long-term planning. One must be ready with an exit plan in case the river overruns the char.

During the pandemic of 2020-2021, MTA devoted its efforts to the design of a prototypical modular mobile structure for the low-income communities living in the chars. As the coronavirus pandemic brought everyday life and activities to a standstill in 2020, Marina Tabassum and her team of architects started working on several design ideas for a mobile dwelling. MTA sought a structural solution that would be easy to assemble and disassemble by the communities themselves with minimal tools. Built with locally sourced materials, it would reduce construction costs in order to make dwellings affordable to ultra-low-income populations. This resulted in the first prototype of the Khudi Bari in June 2020, built by two architects from MTA, Arman Abedin and Kazi Akif Akash. The 8-by-8-foot two-floor prototype cost 250 US dollars. The success of the first structure prompted the team to take Khudi Bari to the next level by reaching out to a char community on the lower Meghna river. Four modular structures were built in the remote location of Char Hijla by MTA's team.

Khudi Bari prototype, Faydabat, Dhaka, 2020

Khudi Bari is a simple spaceframe structure that is made with thick-walled bamboo (Borak) and steel connectors. The structure's rigid frame enables it to withstand the lateral pressure of both wind and water. It has two levels: the ground floor serves as a social and private space, while the upper level provides an area for sleeping and can double as a flood shelter. The lightweight structure requires only a shallow foundation and ground anchors. The roof consists of corrugated metal sheets for ease of transport and maintenance. The facades can be made of any suitable material that is locally available to the community. A finished Khudi Bari with facades looks similar to the vernacular houses existing in the region.

The Khudi Bari is envisioned by MTA as an innovative iteration of the vernacular dwelling. As such, mass acceptance of the structure as climate-resilient is key to the success of the project. This ambitious

→
Khudi Bari, Char Juan Satra, Kurigram, 2022
Photo Afsari Toma/FACE

↓
Khudi Bari in Tanguar Haor, Tahirpur, Shunamganj, 2022
Photo Syntax

attempt required intensive community engagement, knowledge sharing and monitoring of the structure's performance over time. Further research for the Khudi Bari's development required funding and an implementation partner. This led Marina Tabassum to establish the Foundation for Architecture and Community Equity (FACE), which she also chairs with the support of co-chair Khondaker Hasibul Kabir. FACE is an interdisciplinary, not-for-profit organization that focuses on marginalization and displacement in the context of geographically and climatically challenging locations in Bangladesh. The first project to be sponsored by FACE was the implementation of Khudi Bari units. The Swiss Agency for Development and Cooperation awarded a research grant to erect 100 Khudi Baris in various locations in Bangladesh. Khudi Bari projects are now being built by FACE together with volunteers and Bangladeshi communities in areas such as Shunamganj, Kurigram, Rangpur and Jamalpur.

Khudi Bari, Rangpur, 2022
Photo Afsari Toma/FACE

FACE works directly with communities to facilitate processes of co-creation. The community architects orient themselves towards rural and economically disadvantaged populations and mobilize them on site in order to strengthen skills and find autonomous solutions through participatory initiatives. By involving the local population, the architects adhere to the principle of inclusive processes. In this joint undertaking, the professionals take into account the inhabitants' inherent knowledge of the land and vernacular practices, while offering their expertise in regard to spatial organization and contemporary construction methods. The collaboration between the community and the architects can engender sustainable solutions to the current issues of climate crisis.

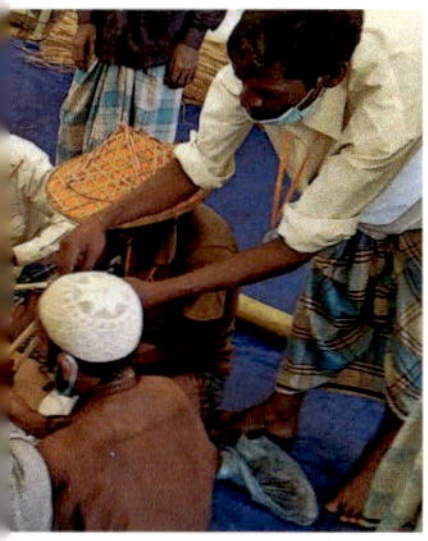

↑
Co-creation workshop, Kutupalong Rohingya refugee camp (8E), Ukhiya Upazila, Cox's Bazar District, 2022
Photo Asif Salman/MTA

The Khudi Bari concept will keep on evolving through time and engagement with different communities. To date, FACE has built houses in various locations, including Tahirpur, Shunamganj and chars in the rivers Teesta, Jamuna and Meghna. MTA has scaled up the Khudi Bari technique and built community centres for women in the Rohingya refugee camps in Ukhiya, as well as Aggregation Centres for women farmers in the host communities of the Teknaf district.

Displacement induced by climatic phenomena is on the rise in Bangladesh, exacerbated by disparities in economic and living conditions. Rising sea levels due to anthropogenic climate change will make the delta considerably more vulnerable in the coming decades, leading to an increase in the number of displaced families. The indefinite transitional state of existence for fellow humans demands attention. There are urgent questions to be asked at a time of growing uncertainty, when adaptation to instability might well be the only remaining strategy. Architecture and design need to expand the agency of precarious populations and focus on basic survival without compromising on the integrity of a good design. Khudi Bari is a step in this direction.

■

↓
Women-Led Community Centre (WLCC), Kutupalong Rohingya refugee camp (8E), Ukhiya Upazila, Cox's Bazar District, 2022
Photo Asif Salman/MTA

Making of Khudi Bari

MARINA TABASSUM

The Khudi Bari was designed with a focus on populations that are being displaced due to both human conflicts and natural disasters – war, persecution, poverty, famine and catastrophic climate change resulting in extreme disparities in the conditions of existence and survival.

The Khudi Bari has several distinctive features:

1. It can be assembled in three days and disassembled in three hours by three to five people. This makes it easy for the homeowners to move from one location to another, especially when faced with extensive soil erosion or a challenge to land occupation without property rights.

2. The main structure of the Khudi Bari is a spaceframe made of bamboo supports and steel connectors. The metal joints and bamboo struts form a stable, robust structure that can withstand the pressure of wind and water.

3. Only a shallow foundation is required.

4. The Khudi Bari has two levels. The ground or plinth level can be used for daily activities and the upper level for sleeping. The upper level can also serve as a refuge during flood season.

5. Khudi Bari is envisioned as an innovative iteration of vernacular architecture; consequently, a completed house looks similar to the traditional local houses.

6. Materials are sourced locally to simplify the supply chain and reduce costs. Preference is given to natural, renewable materials from the area.

"As I sat in my silent office during the pandemic, this image of a house flashed through my mind and I thought: This is it! A simple house that is affordable for a propertyless family and can be transported from one place to another. This is how the journey of Khudi Bari started."

MARINA TABASSUM

↓
Construction of a Khudi Bari, Char Juan Satra, Kurigram, Teesta River, 2022

7. The building cost of a single Khudi Bari unit is 450 US dollars, including transport and labour (status July 2023).

(→ p. 39)

8. The Khudi Bari structure can be scaled up by combining several modules, which are suited for use as community centres, schools and other communal facilities. One such example is the women's centre in the Rohingya refugee camp in Ukhiya, Cox's Bazar.

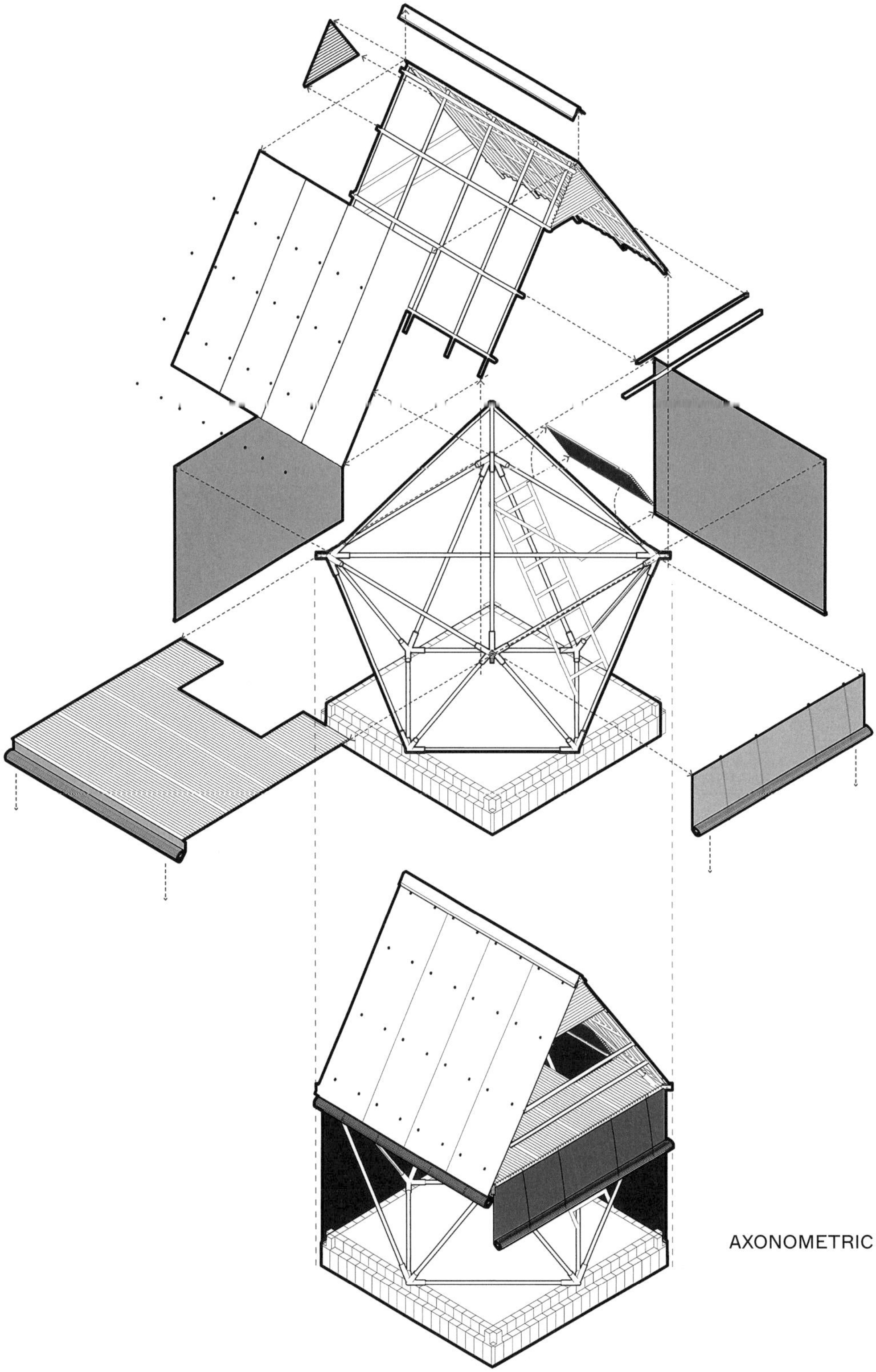

AXONOMETRIC

FOR STRUCTURE

BORAK BAMBOO

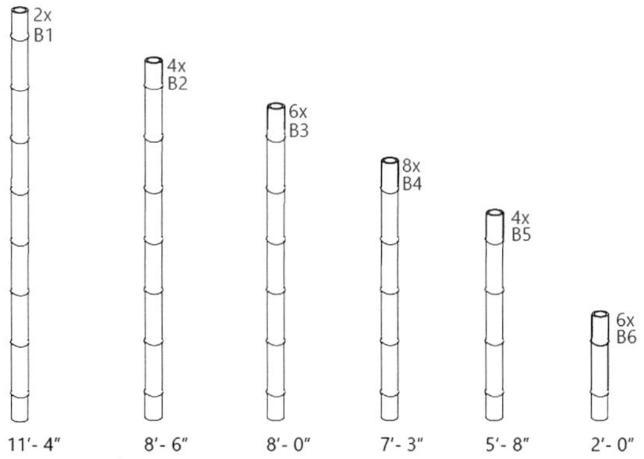

FOR STRUCTURE

STEEL JOINTS

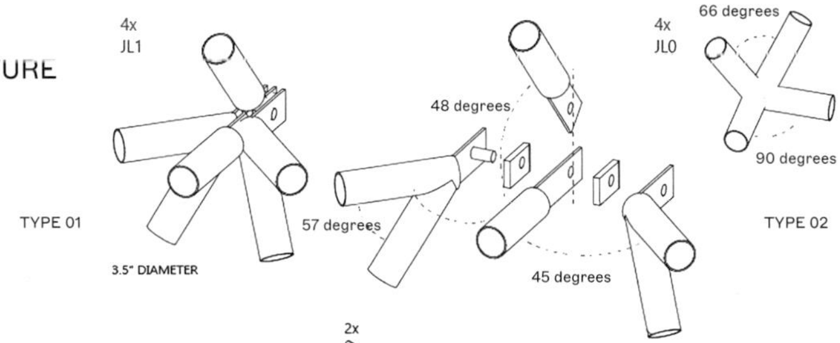

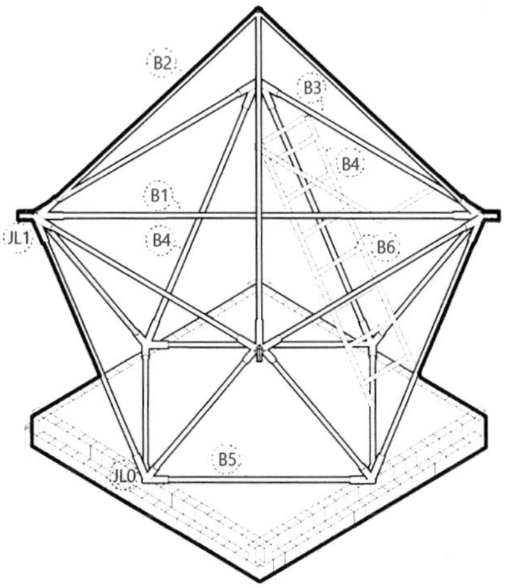

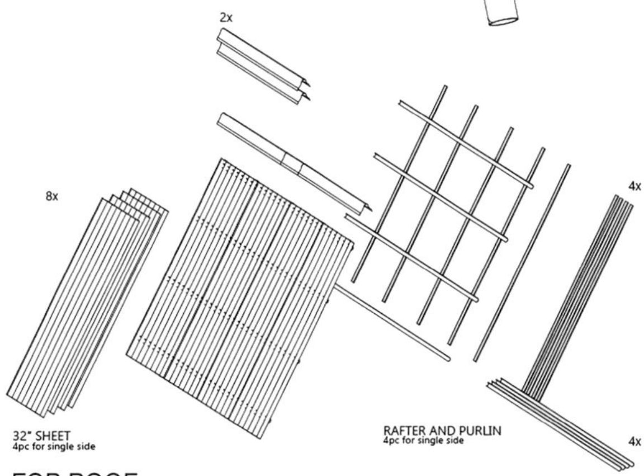

FOR ROOF

CORRUGATED SHEET METAL AND SPLIT BAMBOO

COSTS	
BAMBOO	BDT 4000/ USD 48
STEEL JOINTS	BDT 8000/ USD 95
CORRUGATED SHEET (TIN)	BDT 2600/ USD 31
UPPER SHEET (TIN)	BDT 400 / USD 5
NUT - BOLT	BDT 900 / USD 11
ROPE	BDT 100 / USD 2
	BDT 1600 / USD 190 Approx

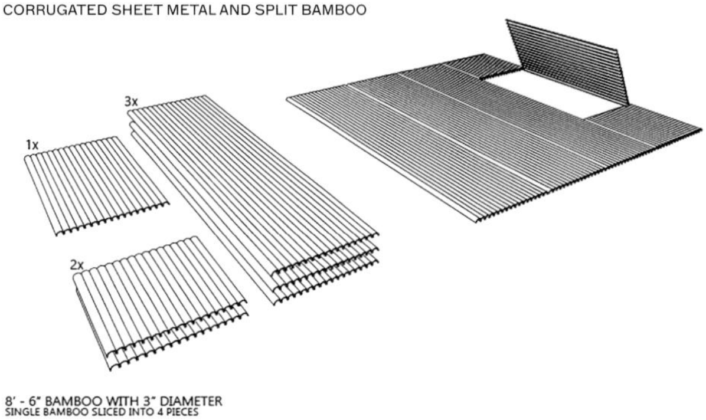

FOR FLOOR (MACHA – LEVEL 01)

SPLIT BAMBOO

Construction of Khudi Bari

For the construction of a Khudi Bari, culms of Borak bamboo are required in several different lengths. Borak bamboo is sourced from the northern part of Bangladesh and has a high tensile strength, making it well suited for structural applications. Steel connectors were designed by MTA to join the bamboo struts together in a spaceframe structure.

Upon completion of the frame, the community can focus on making the foundation. Concrete poles with a length of 75 cm are driven into the sand. The steel connectors for the bottom level of the Khudi Bari are affixed to the short piles. Then a mud plinth is built over the bottom layer to stabilize the structure.

Once the spaceframe has been erected on the site, the wooden platform of the upper floor is assembled. In the next step, the rafters and purlins are joined to the Khudi Bari's structural members, followed by the attachment of the corrugated metal sheeting for the gable roof. After the roof is in place, the triangular facades with operable openings are affixed on two sides of the upper floor.

This completes the basic Khudi Bari dwelling. The homeowners have the option of enclosing the lower floor with an available and affordable facade material, potentially including doors. In order to make larger structures, several Khudi Bari modules can be connected to each other with additional steel joints and bamboo struts.

(→ pp. 52–55)

■

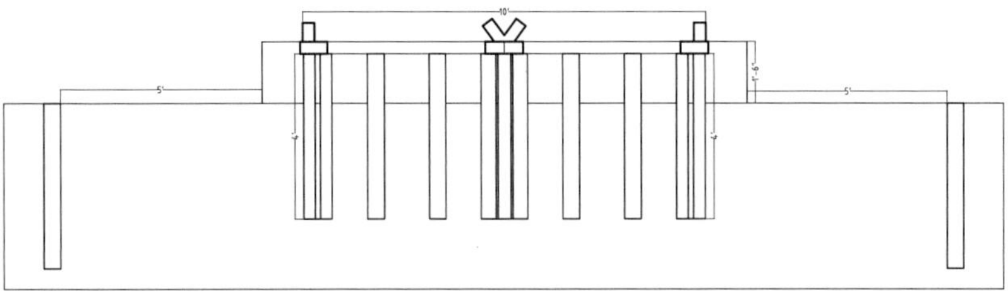

Step-01

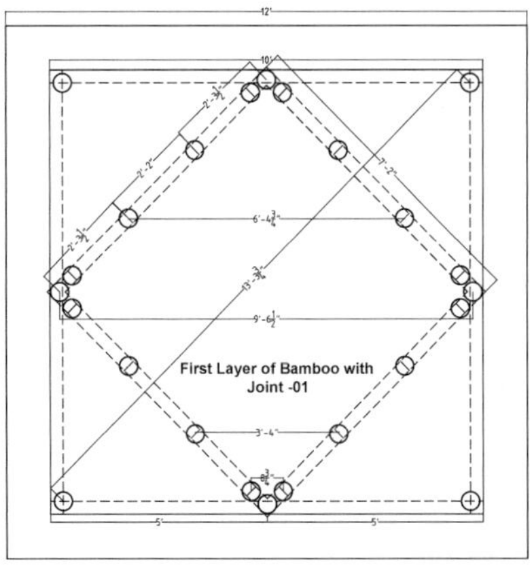

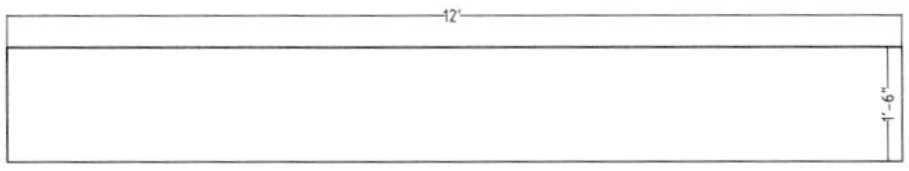

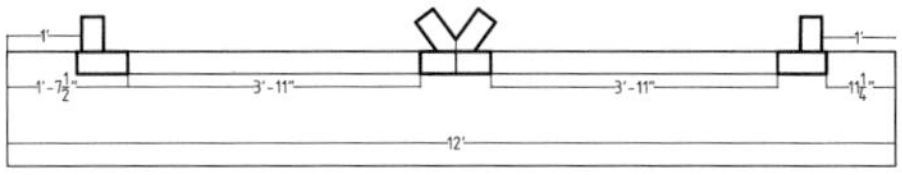

Step-02

Step-03

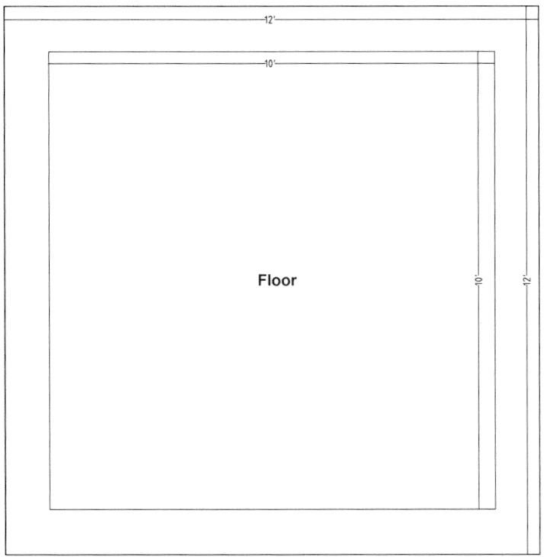

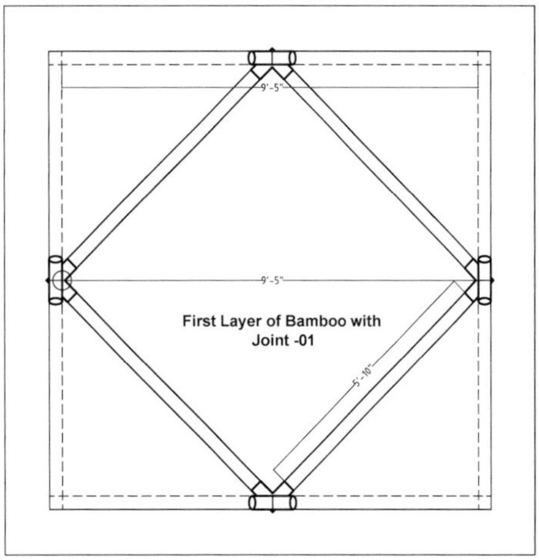

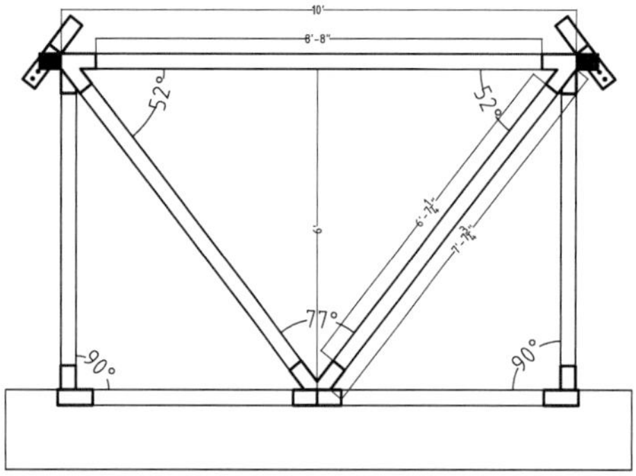

Step-04

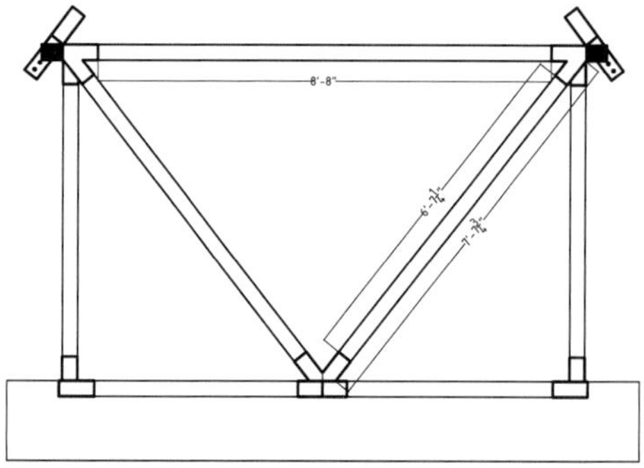

Step-05

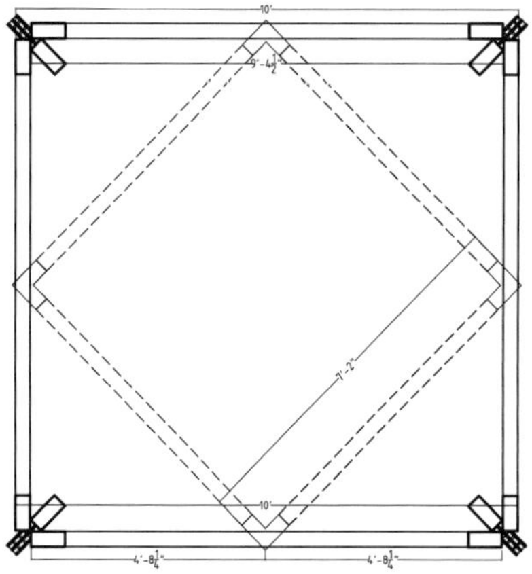

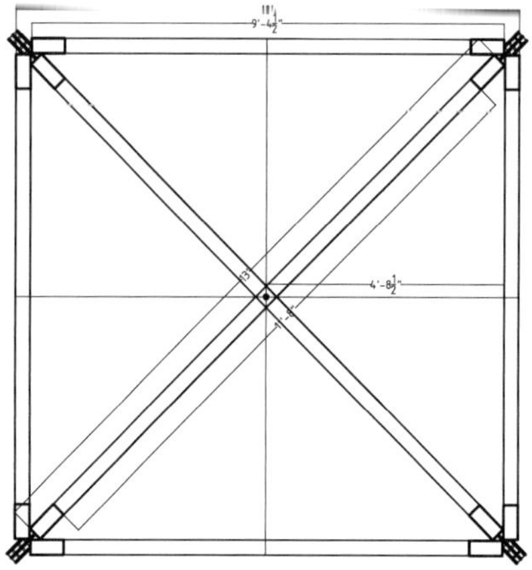

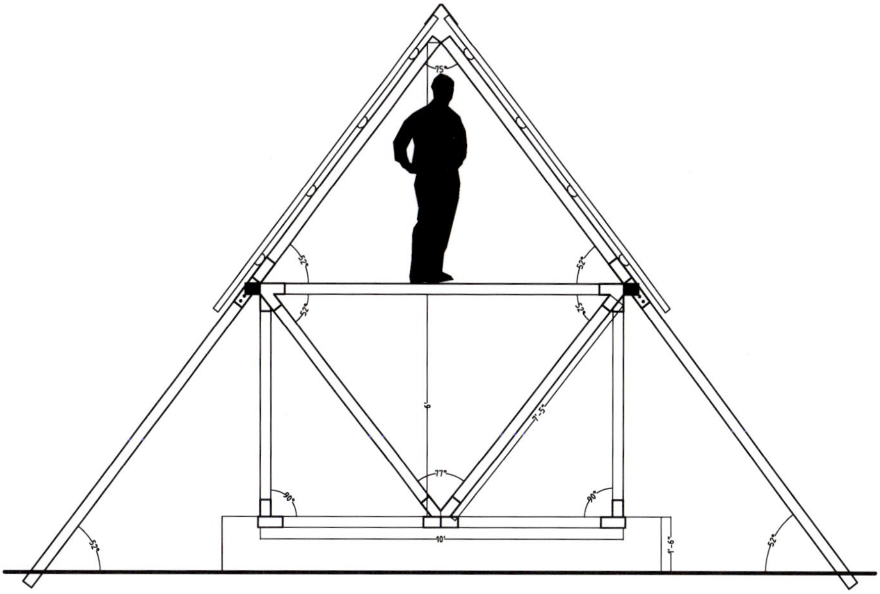

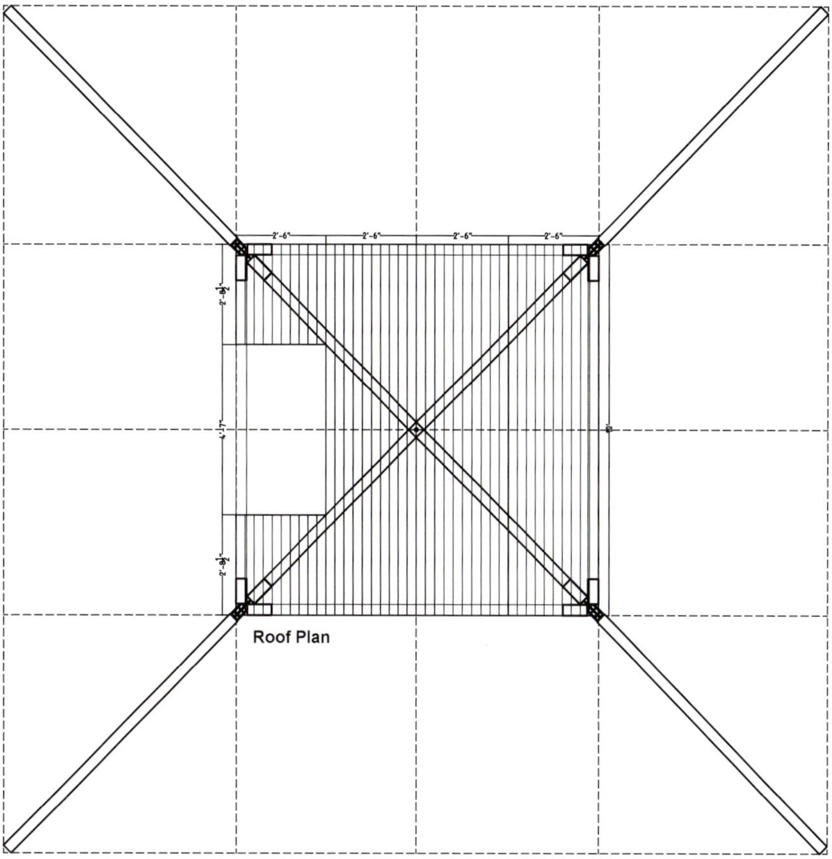

Roof Plan

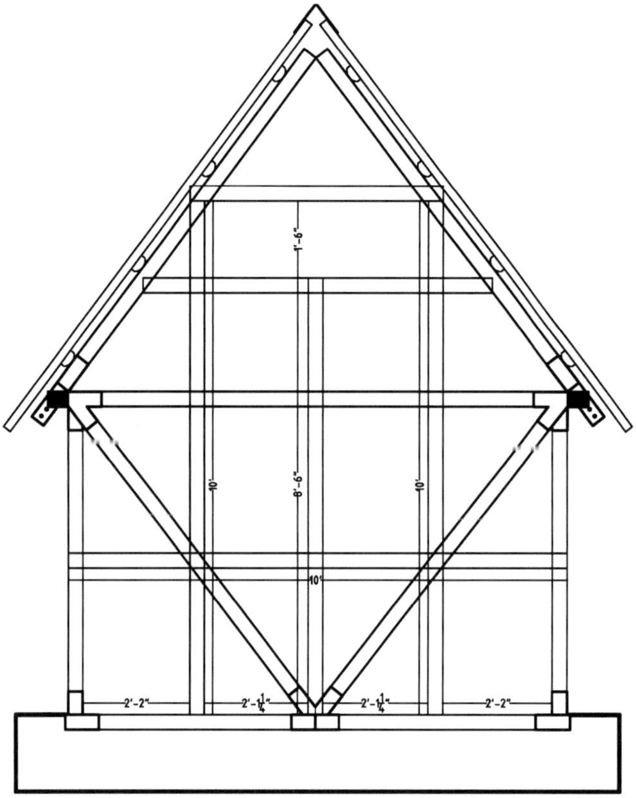

ELEVATION

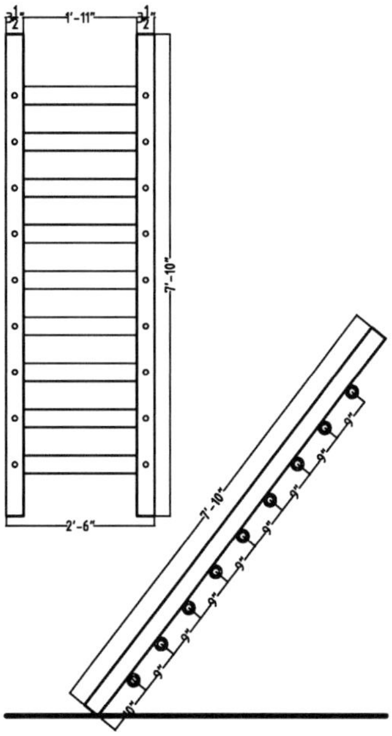

STAIR

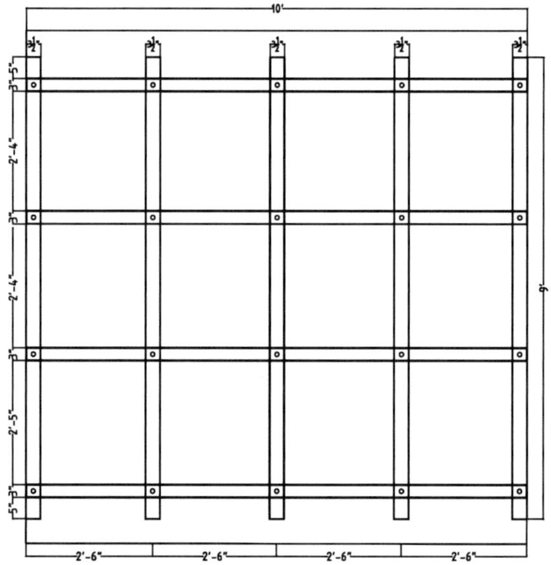

ROOF FRAME (SLICED BAMBOO / BETEL)

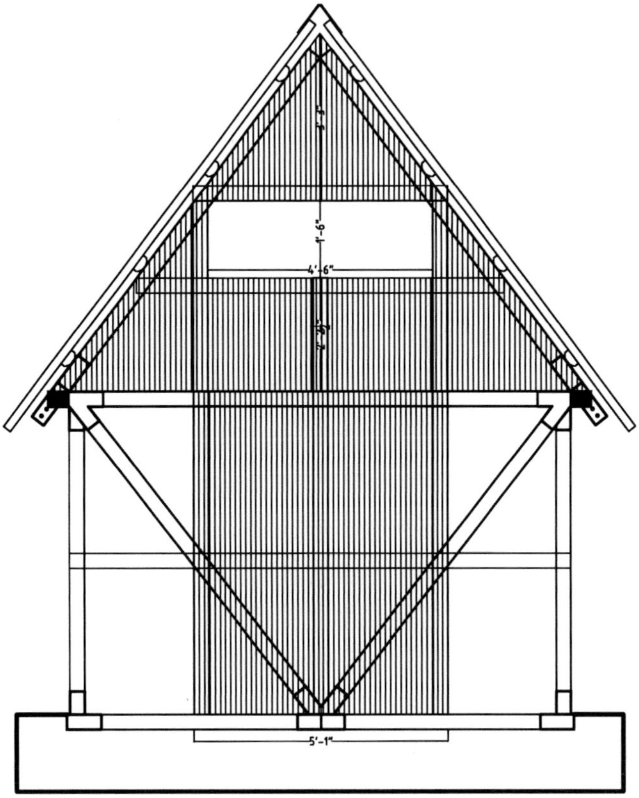

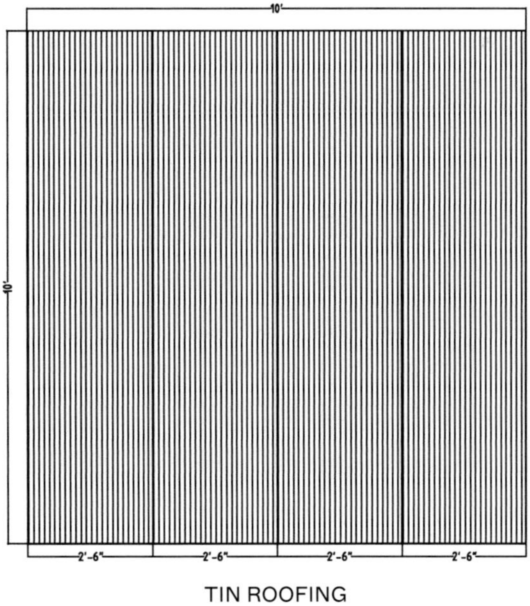

TIN ROOFING

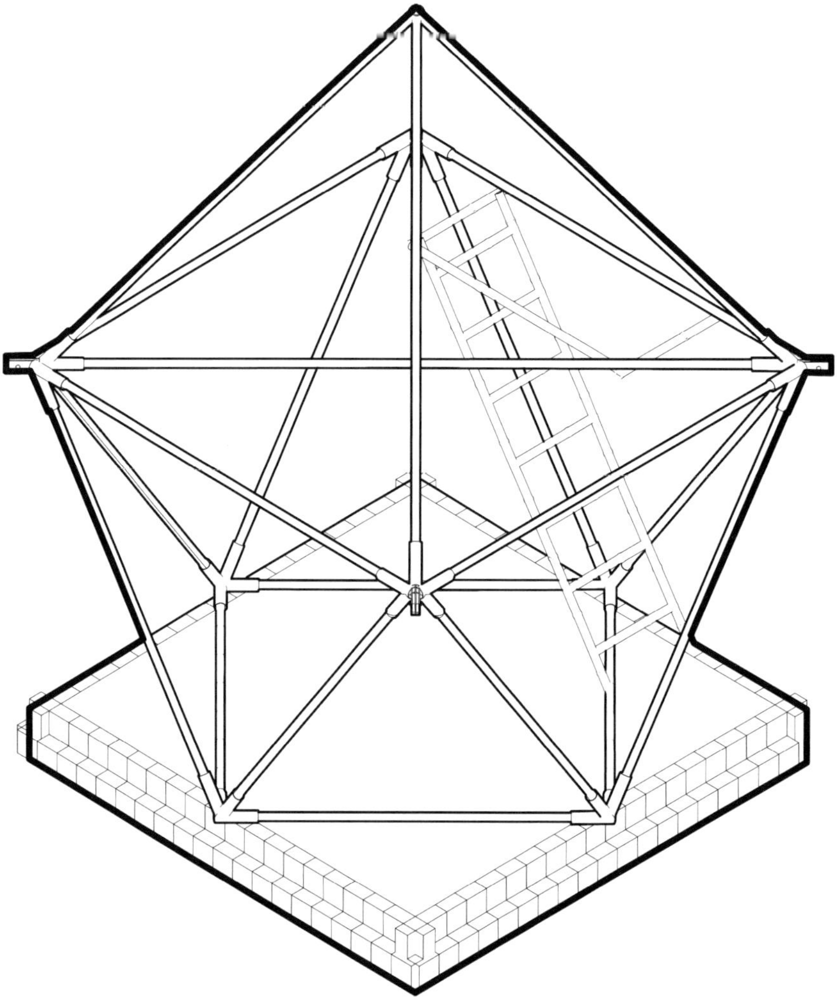

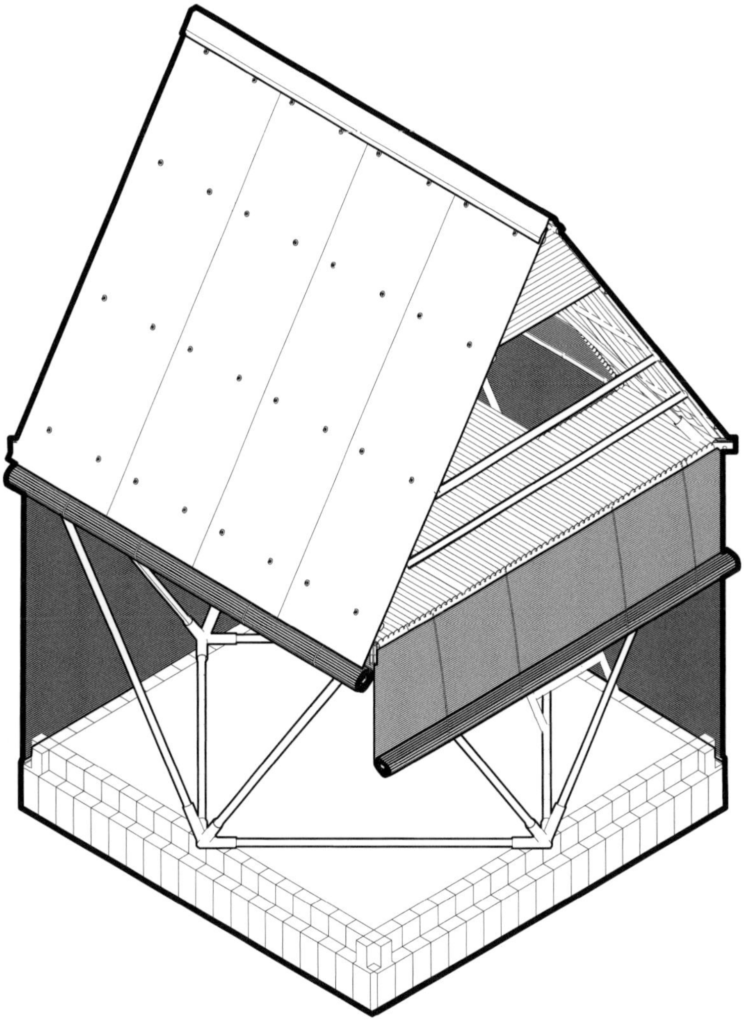

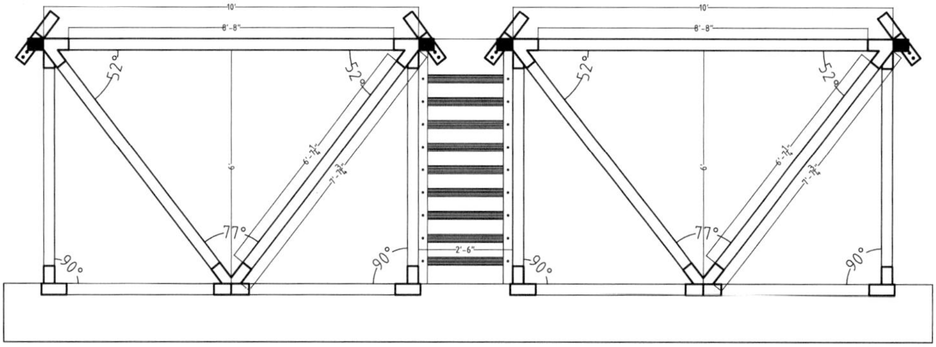

House-B Section

Step-04B

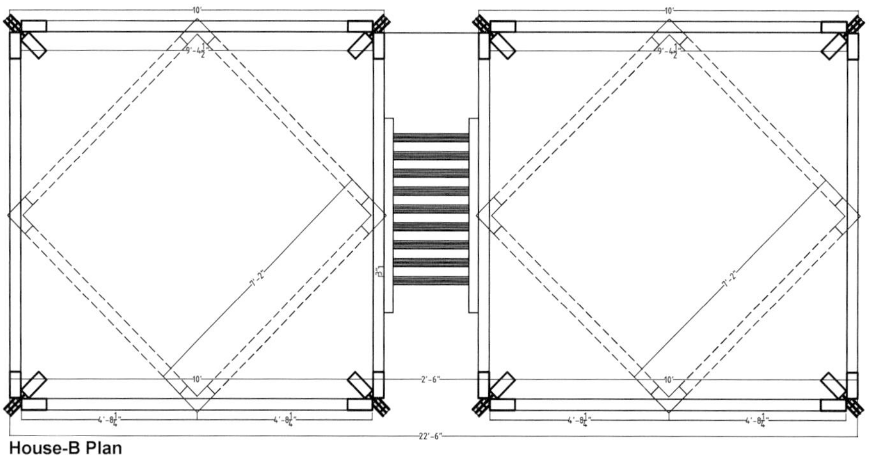

House-B Plan

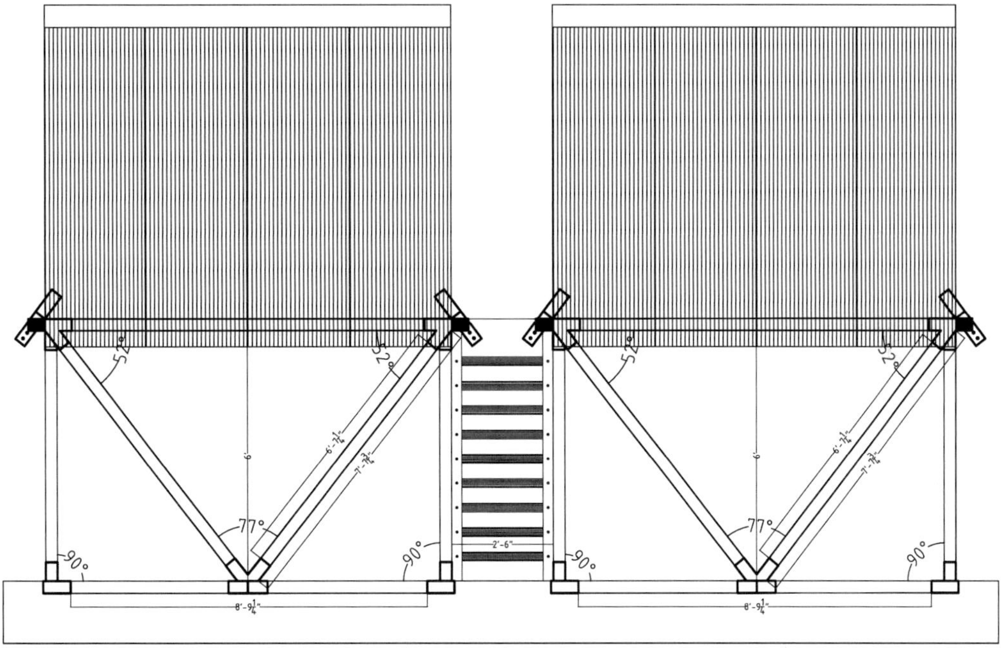

House-B Section

Step-07B

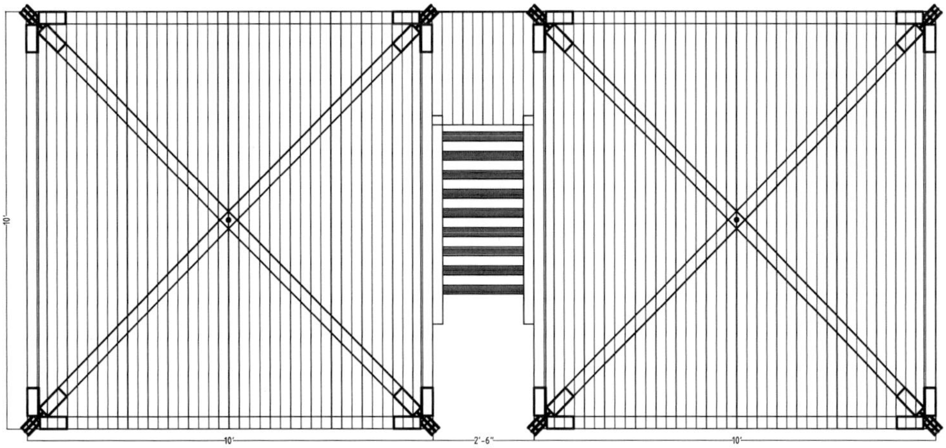

House-B Plan

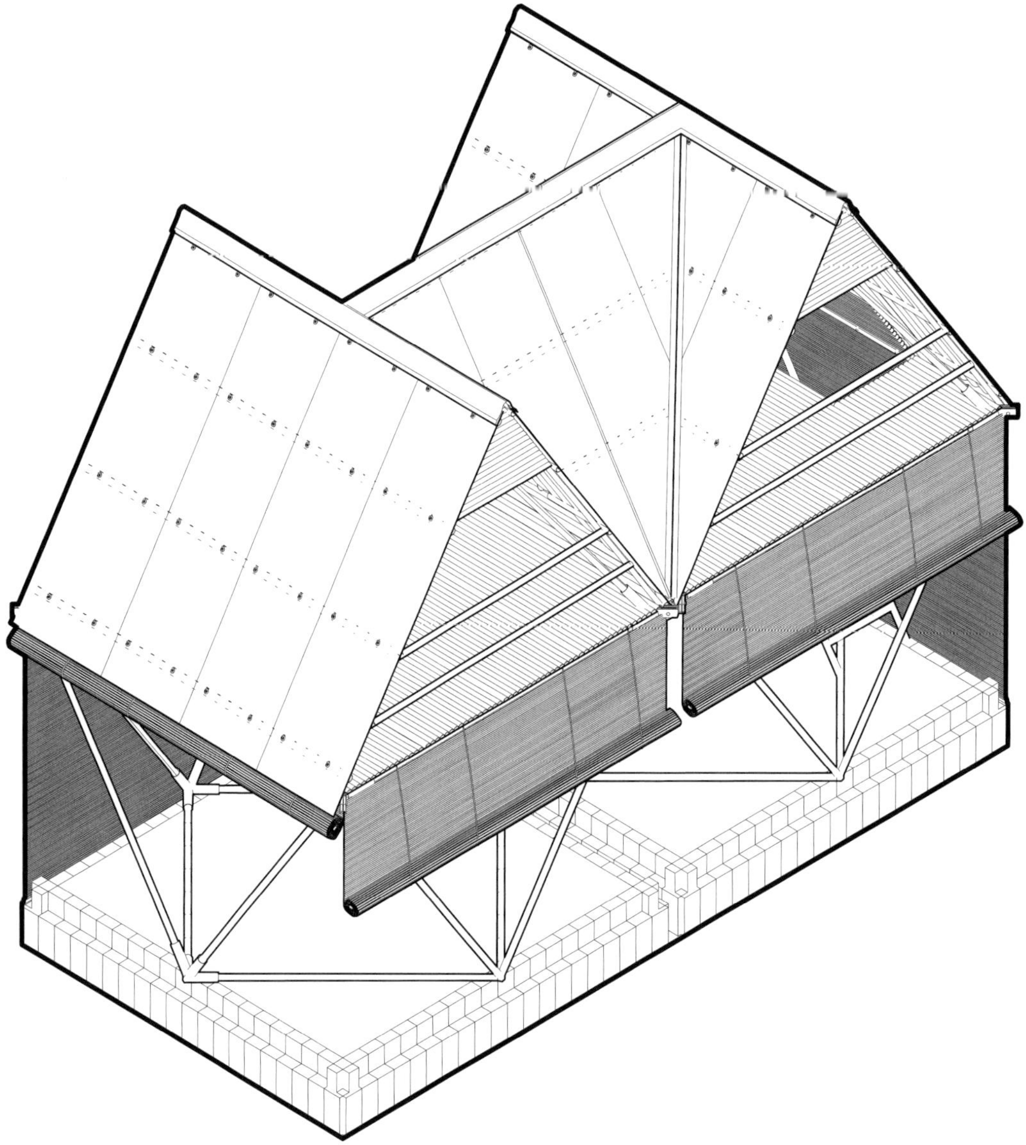

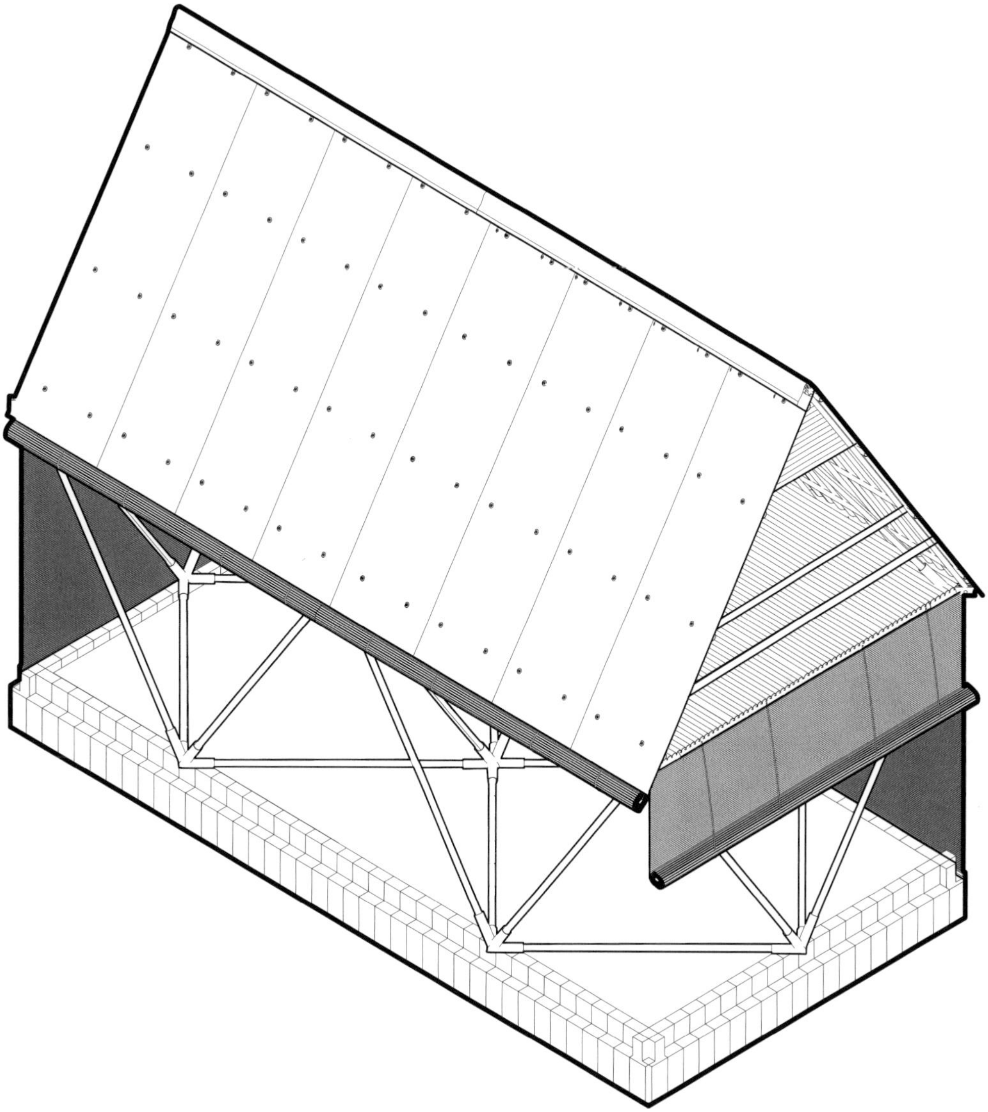

PART ONE of the Khudi Bari journey: Preparation in Dhaka

ARMAN ABEDIN

Located in the garden on the Vitra Campus, the Khudi Bari is exposed to the natural elements of rain, sun and snow. All of the building materials were sourced from Bangladesh and are similar to the original materials used for the Khudi Baris erected on the riverine sandbars (chars) of the Bengal delta. Our main concern was how the bamboo would perform in Germany's cold winter weather.

For that reason, we selected the type of bamboo with great care. The bamboos were sourced from Jashore, where Panigram Resort is located, an eco-tourism project by MTA. The architect Argha Shaha, project manager of the resort, handpicked the bamboo culms. Upon harvesting they were submerged in a water tank to wash away the sap and prevent insect attacks. After two weeks of this treatment, the bamboos were left in the open air to dry. Then they were packed on site at Panigram and sent to MTA's office in Dhaka.

The wood for timber components was sourced from a market in Dohar near Dhaka.

The steel connectors for the spaceframe were made by Akhtaruzzaman of Mamun Engineering Works in Dhaka. He has produced all of the connectors for the Khudi Baris built to date, making him an expert. The joints were fabricated from steel pipe, and in anticipation of the winter rain in Germany, a thermal coating was applied especially for Vitra. The connectors were packed by MTA.

All of the construction materials were brought from different places to MTA's office in Dhanmondi, Dhaka, where they were prepared for shipping, loaded onto a truck and hauled to Chittagong for sea transport.

■

BUNDLE

PART TWO of the Khudi Bari journey: Arrival in Weil am Rhein and construction on the Vitra Campus

CHRISTIAN GERMADNIK

The entire consignment of Khudi Bari building materials was shipped in February 2024 by cargo vessel from the port of Chittagong in Bangladesh to Rotterdam, from where it was delivered by land to Weil am Rhein at the end of March 2024. Upon arrival at the Vitra Campus, it was discovered that mildew had formed on the surface of several bamboo components, due to the humid and warm conditions in the container during sea transport. After a drying period of roughly five weeks, the layer of mildew was removed without any residue – the parts were now ready for assembly.

As bamboo is not a certified building product in Europe, the construction of the Khudi Bari on the Vitra Campus initially posed a minor challenge for the German engineering firm responsible for the construction plans. However, the structural stability of the design was confirmed. The Khudi Bari framework is attached to a concrete foundation with flat steel flanges welded to the steel joints at the base.

Working with bamboo was also an unfamiliar task for the local carpenters. To answer their questions during the building phase, Arman Abedin, the architect from Marina Tabassum's studio who had supervised the construction of Khudi Baris in Bangladesh, was present during the entire process of preparing and assembling the timber components.

Once the load-bearing bamboo structure was completed, the next step was to install the corrugated metal roof. Then the gable ends were closed off with panels made of sheet metal. Cross ventilation in the upper storey is facilitated by window openings and fixed wooden slats on both facades.

In the case of the Khudi Baris in Bangladesh, family life takes place mostly outdoors. The aim on the Vitra Campus was to enable visitors to experience this as well. Marina Tabassum designed the exterior elements and landscaping. The area beneath and around the Khudi Bari was paved with bricks left over from renovations on the neighbouring factory building by Álvaro Siza. Two stationary benches were made out of the same brick material. The excess bamboo cane was used to construct a long bamboo table and four bamboo benches based on designs by Marina Tabassum. Together with a drinking fountain, the ensemble invites visitors to linger and relax.

The Khudi Bari was inaugurated on 12 June 2024 in conjunction with the Vitra Campus Summer Party and has been accessible to the public ever since.

■

D-TEC
GER GA 315

→

→

→

→

PART TWO of the Khudi Bari journey: Arrival in Weil am Rhein and construction on the Vitra Campus

PROJECT MEMBERS

ARCHITECT
Marina Tabassum Architects
(Marina Tabassum, Arman Abedin)

PROJECT MANAGEMENT
Logad GmbH
(Christian Germadnik,
Abel Rodríguez Rico)

STRUCTURAL ENGINEERS
Ingenieurbüro Autenrieth –
Ingenieurgesellschaft mbH
(Matthias Autenrieth)

SURVEYING
Ingenieurbüro Bölk und Gantner GmbH

TIMBER CONSTRUCTION
Holzbau Blum GmbH

MASONRY
Binder & Blum GmbH

EARTHWORKS, FOUNDATIONS
AND LANDSCAPING
Albert Blauel Hausmeisterservice

SANITARY SYSTEMS
Wolfgang Armbruster GmbH

METALWORK
Jehnich Metall- & Messebau GmbH

PAINTWORK
Die Malermeister Beckert GmbH

IMAGE CREDITS

Unless explicitly stated, all photographs and other illustrations were produced and provided by Marina Tabassum Architects.

pp. 70–71, 74–75 and cover bottom right, photos: Iwan Baan • pp. 64–69, 72–73, 76–77 and inside back cover © Vitra, photos: Julien Lanoo • pp. 60, 62–63, photos: Christian Germadnik and team •

Every effort was made to accurately state the source or author of the images. Any errors or omissions are unintentional and will be corrected in future editions.

Editor: Rolf Fehlbaum
Copy editing: Barbara Hauss

Graphic design: Thorsten Romanus
Production management: Nadine Kessler
Distribution: Pinar Yildiz
Printing: DZA Druckerei zu Altenburg GmbH
Paper: Magno Volume 150 and 250 g/qm
Typeface: ABC Marfa, IBM Plex Mono

Second edition, 2025
First published by the Vitra Design Museum, 2024

Vitra Design Museum
Charles-Eames-Str. 2
79576 Weil am Rhein
Germany
verlag@design-museum.de
www.design-museum.de

Printed and bound in Germany

The German National Library has listed this publication in the German National Bibliography; detailed bibliographical data is available at http://dnb.dnb.de

ISBN 978-3-945852-67-5